★★
★The Library of
American Landmarks

THE HOOVER DAM

Patra McSharry Sevastiades

The Rosen Publishing Group's
PowerKids Press™
New York

Published in 1997 by The Rosen Publishing Group, Inc.
29 East 21st Street, New York, NY 10010

Copyright © 1997 by The Rosen Publishing Group, Inc.

First Edition

Book design: Danielle Primiceri

Photo credits: Cover, pp. 4, 7, 17, 19 © Image Bank; p. 11 © Keystone-Underwood/FPG International; pp. 8–9, 14 © UPI/Corbis-Bettmann; p. 13 © AP/Wide World Photos; p. 16–17 © The Bettmann Archive; p. 20 (top) © Wilson North/International Stock; p. 20 (bottom) © Bettmann.

Sevastiades, Patra McSharry.
    The Hoover Dam / Patra McSharry Sevastiades.
        p.   cm. — (The Library of American landmarks)
    Includes index.
    Summary: Briefly describes the process involved in building the Hoover Dam.
    ISBN 0-8239-5021-2
    1. Hoover Dam (Ariz. and Nev.)—History—Juvenile literature. [1. Hoover Dam (Ariz. and Nev.)—Design and construction. 2. Dams—Designs and construction.] I. Title. II. Series.
    TC557.3.H6S48 1997
    627'.82—dc21   97-5861
                                                                                                                         CIP
                                                                                                                         AC

Manufactured in the United States of America

Table of Contents

1 Controlling the Colorado River   5

2 What Is a Dam?   6

3 The Home of the Hoover Dam   9

4 Building Boulder City   10

5 Moving the River   12

6 Getting the Canyon Ready   15

7 Pouring and Cooling the Concrete   16

8 Making a Lake   18

9 The Dam Is Opened   21

10 An Amazing Dam   22

   Glossary   23

   Index   24

Controlling the Colorado River

For thousands of years, the Colorado River helped the lives of people, plants, and animals that lived near it. But the river was also dangerous. Sometimes it **flooded** (FLUD-ed) nearby towns. Other times it dried up, causing **droughts** (DROWTS). During droughts, people, plants, and animals didn't have enough water to stay alive. By the early 1900s, people began to look for a way to control the mighty Colorado River. In 1902, a team of scientists who studied the river thought that building a dam would work.

◀ Today, the Colorado River provides millions of people with water and power.

What Is a Dam?

A dam is a **structure** (STRUK-sher) that controls the flow of water in a river. The scientists who studied the Colorado River knew that building a dam would keep the river from flooding. It would also help to bring water to the fields where farmers grew their crops. A dam could bring water to towns and cities that needed it. And the movement of the water through the dam could even make **electricity** (ee-lek-TRIH-sih-tee). Most people agreed that building a dam was a good idea. In 1928, the U.S. Congress set aside money to build the Hoover Dam.

The Hoover Dam was first ▶ called the Boulder Dam.

The Home of the Hoover Dam

Scientists decided that the best place to build the Hoover Dam was where the Colorado River flowed through the Black Canyon in the states of Nevada and Arizona. It took many **engineers** (en-jin-EERZ) and 3,500 workers to design and build it. The workers started building in 1931, and finished five years later, in 1936. That was two years earlier than anyone expected the dam to be finished!

◀ When the Hoover Dam was built, it was the tallest dam in the world.

Building Boulder City

At first, the workers camped out by the **dam site** (DAM SYT). But Black Canyon is in the middle of the desert. In the desert, it can get as hot as 119° F during the summer. The workers did not have enough water to drink or to wash and keep clean. Many of them became sick. So a town was built for the workers to live in. It was called Boulder City. Today, 14,000 people live in Boulder City.

Boulder City was built for the Hoover Dam workers. Today, it is the city with the most land in Nevada. ▶

Moving the River

To build the Hoover Dam, engineers first had to move the Colorado River away from the place where the workers planned to build. To do this, workers used **dynamite** (DY-nuh-myt). They blasted four tunnels in the walls of Black Canyon, nearly a mile away from the area where they wanted to build. The tunnels worked. The river water flowed through the tunnels and around the dam site. Now the workers had nearly one mile of dry ground on which to work.

After the four tunnels were built, it took less than 24 hours for workers to force the Colorado River to ▶ flow through the tunnels.

Getting the Canyon Ready

After the water was moved, there was a thick layer of mud on the floor of the dam site. Workers removed the mud until they reached a hard **surface** (SER-fuss) called **bedrock** (BED-rok). Other workers helped to make the canyon ready to work in. Their job was to remove any loose rocks from the canyon walls. The workers were hung from ropes that hung down the sides of the canyon. Once the canyon was safe, the workers were ready to build. It was time to pour the **concrete** (kon-KREET).

◀ Workers had to dig into the river bed to begin building the dam.

Pouring and Cooling the Concrete

As concrete hardens, it lets off heat. If the concrete for the Hoover Dam had been poured all at once, it would have taken more than 100 years to cool! And the dam would have cracked as the concrete cooled. The engineers realized that they needed to pour the concrete for the dam in large blocks, or piece by piece. The engineers also had workers lay one-inch steel pipes in the hardening concrete. They ran cold water through these pipes to cool it even faster.

The concrete of the Hoover Dam cooled in less than two years without cracking. ▶

The water cooled the concrete much faster than if the concrete had cooled on its own. Later, the pipes were filled with **grout** (GROWT), which made the dam even stronger.

Making a Lake

Workers also built **intake towers** (IN-tayk TOW-erz) behind the wall of the dam. These towers can be opened and closed. They allow water to enter large pipes that lead to the bottom of the dam. The towers were left closed until the dam was finished.

Now the workers were ready for the river. They closed the four tunnels in the walls of Black Canyon. River water began to flow into the dam site again. Behind the wall of the dam, a lake began to form. The new lake was named Lake Mead.

Lake Mead stretches for over 100 miles. This is the end that's closest to the dam. ▶

The Dam Is Opened

Meanwhile, at the foot of the dam, workers built **powerhouses** (POW-er-how-sez). Each powerhouse contained several **electrical generators** (ee-LEK-trih-kul JEN-er-ay-terz). The dam was almost finished!

On September 11, 1936, the dam began to work. The intake towers were opened, and water from Lake Mead entered them. The water flowed into pipes that led to the powerhouses. The water moved through the generators in each powerhouse. As it passed through each generator, the water created electricity.

◄ The water flows from the Colorado River, into Lake Mead, through the dam, and becomes the Colorado River again.

An Amazing Dam

The dam worked very well. It kept the Colorado River from flooding. It created electricity for Arizona, Nevada, and southern California. It also changed the way people thought about the western United States. The land had once been dry and hard to live on. Now there was plenty of water for everyone. In 1947, the dam was named the Hoover Dam for former President Herbert Hoover. President Hoover had been a great supporter of building the dam. The Hoover Dam still works well today. It is known as one of the seven wonders of the **modern** (MOH-dern) world.

Glossary

bedrock (BED-rok) The layer of solid rock below dirt and loose rock.

concrete (kon-KREET) A hard, strong building material.

dam site (DAM SYT) The place where a dam will be built.

drought (DROWT) A long time without rain or water.

dynamite (DY-nuh-myt) A powerful explosive.

electrical generator (ee-LEK-trih-kul JEN-er-ay-ter) A machine that can turn the movement of water into electricity.

electricity (ee-lek-TRIH-sih-tee) A kind of energy.

engineer (en-jin-EER) A person who designs or builds structures.

flood (FLUD) To overflow with water.

grout (GROWT) A pasty mix of a solid material and water that hardens and is used to fill spaces.

intake tower (IN-tayk TOW-er) A tall, tower-shaped drain behind a dam.

modern (MOH-dern) Having to do with modern times.

powerhouse (POW-er-hows) A building that contains electrical generators.

structure (STRUK-sher) Something that is built.

surface (SER-fuss) The top layer.

Index

B
bedrock, 15
Black Canyon, 9,
10, 12, 18
Boulder City; 10

C
Colorado River, 5,
6, 9, 12, 22
concrete, 14, 16, 17
crops, 6

D
desert, 10
droughts, 5
dynamite, 12

E
electrical generators,
21

electricity, 6, 21,
22
engineers, 9, 12,
16

F
flooding, 5, 6, 22

H
Hoover, President
Herbert, 22

I
intake towers, 18,
21

L
Lake Mead, 18, 21

P
powerhouses, 21

S
scientists, 5, 6, 9

T
tunnels, 12, 18

U
U.S. Congress, 6

W
workers, 9, 10, 12,
15, 18, 21

MAI

GAYLORD FG